The Schneider Trophy

Alan Smith

Published by
Waterfront Publications
An Imprint of Bookmark International
Alpha House, Launceston, Cornwall, PL15 9HT. Telephone 01566 772709, Fax 01566 776061
Printed by Amadeus Press, Huddersfield, West Yorkshire

Foreword

This book revisits the Schneider Trophy contests, arguably aviation's greatest, using contemporary photographs and personal recollections. Many of the pictures have never been published before.

This book does not set out to retell the Schneider story in detail – there are a number of books by various authors which are still available which do this and readers should refer to the bibliography at the back. Instead, the pictures and memories describe the progression from the wood-and-fabric biplanes which competed in the early contests, to the sleek, all-metal high-speed racers which characterised the final races.

The final two contests, both held from the RAF flying boat station at Calshot in Hampshire, form the focus of this book. This is inevitable, since the surviving veterans were naturally involved with these later events, held in 1929 and 1931. But it is also appropriate to concentrate on these final two years, because, whilst 1991 marked the Diamond Jubilee of Great Britain's final permanent retention of the Schneider Trophy, this new edition recognises the continuing interest in the subject. The legend lives on!

An Introduction to the Schneider Trophy

Jacques Schneider announced the rules for his new aviation contest at the dinner of the 1912 Gordon Bennett Aviation Cup, one of a number of contests for aeroplanes which were held in the early years of the century.

These early contests, underwritten by wealthy individuals or businessmen, were designed to prod the development of the aeroplane, to provoke excitement in a new form of transport, and as often as not to generate publicity for the sponsor.

Schneider's new Trophy was different – it was for seaplanes only. His view was that, with about two thirds of the earth's surface covered with water, and with most major cities served either by rivers or sea ports, the development of the seaplane should be encouraged so that it became an effective means of global transportation.

To this end, he offered La Coupe d'Aviation Maritime Jacques Schneider, valued at £1,000. It was to be the main award for an annual event held between national aero clubs, rather than individual pilots (another difference from the other contests at the time). Each club was allowed a maximum of three entries, and the winning club organised the following year's contest, with the inevitable home advantage. Prize money of £1,000 was also offered for each of the first three contests. Keen not to encourage freak aircraft, the rules stipulated that the contests take place over the open sea, over a course at least 150 nautical miles long. There were two parts to each contest: a speed trial, with aircraft competing against the clock, and a seaworthiness trial.

Finally, any country winning the Trophy three times in five years (amended to three times in five contests after the 1927 contest) would retain the Trophy permanently.

These were the rules as originally set out by Schneider and his advisers. Over the years they were modified, both as a consequence of aeroplane development and as different national aero clubs requested changes. The initial prize money was soon used up, but the competitions had by then grown in prestige to such an extent that winning the Schneider Trophy was enough.

The seaworthiness tests were originally designed to counteract the development of pure racers, and comprised navigability and mooring tests. Over the years, though, they became less stringent, and by the time of the final contests were simply taxying and alighting trials.

In fact, the character of Schneider's contests changed considerably over the years they were run, and their importance on the development of aircraft was different from that which he originally envisaged. The flying boat was to reign supreme in the years immediately before the Second World War, primarily with Imperial Airways and Pan American, reflecting Schneider's vision. But the reasons for this were as much that modern developments such as variable pitch propellers, flaps and effective breaking systems, were only being developed from the mid-1930s, and seaplanes could make use of the large stretches of water available to them to take off and land. Certainly, the Schneider Trophy had no influence on any of the commercial flying boats concurrently in use. It was the development of the bomber during the Second World War which gave designers the techniques required for producing large land aircraft in peace time and the flying boat then became obsolete. The Schneider Trophy contests instead became technology development contests. The need for increased speed led the designers away from useful flying boats to racers whose payloads were one pilot and fuel, and whose engines had lives of little over one hour. The result was the accelerated development of aero engines, streamlining, fuel, reliability and, to a smaller extent, an increased understanding of the medical effects of high speed flying on pilots.

This was, of course, at odds with Schneider's original intent. But the contests became a symbol for prestige and excellence in aviation, they excited the general public in a way difficult to imagine today, and they resulted in the development of the fastest objects on the planet.

Part One: 1913-1927

Above: A Morane-Saulnier at Monaco in 1913. This is the same type of aircraft entered for the first Schneider Trophy contest by Roland Garros. To whom the aeroplane in the picture actually belongs is uncertain. According to the available references Garros' aircraft had race number 2, so this would seem not to be his. However, his was the only Morane monoplane at the 1913 Monaco meeting. Perhaps the number was changed. The first Schneider Trophy contest was organised by the Aéro-Club de France at Monaco in 1913, as part of a much larger hydro-aero-plane meeting. Contemporary reports of the event pay little interest to the Schneider contest. Garros finished second in his Morane, which was powered by a 80hp Gnome engine. The contest was won by another Frenchman, Maurice Prévost, flying a Déperdussin. This was the only time the French won the Schneider Trophy. *Quadrant picture library*

Right: The Italian pilot Guido Jannello flying his Savoia S.13 over Bourne-mouth Bay in the 1919 contest. This was the first contest after the First World War and the course was a triangle with turning points at Christ-church Bay, Bournemouth Pier and at Swanage Bay. The yacht is the Royal Aero Club's base for the contest. The whole contest was plagued by foggy weather and indifferent organisation. Communication between the pilots, based on Bournemouth beach, and the organisers on the yacht was poor. Jannello was the only pilot to fly the course in the poor weather. However, it was discovered after the contest that he had not turned round the Swanage marker boat, but its reserve moored close by. As such he had not completed the course and was disqualified. Considerable exchanges followed, with Jannello being reinstated for a while. Ultimately, the Fédér-ation Aéronautique Internationale (aviation's international sporting body, then and now) ruled the event void, but awarded Italy the right to stage the next year's contest. *Quadrant picture library*

The Supermarine Sea Lion I, of 1919. This was the first aircraft entered by Supermarine for a Schneider Trophy contest. It was a modified Sea King, itself a modification of the war time Baby aircraft. It was powered by a 450hp Napier Lion engine (hence the aircraft's name) and was flown in the contest by Squadron Leader Basil Hobbs. The designer who carried out the modifications was the young R.J. Mitchell. In comparison with the later aircraft which competed in the Schneider Trophy contests, the early flying boats may appear clumsy aircraft. But close study of this picture shows that, in fact, it was quite graceful in its design. In the contest, Hobbs hit a submerged object whilst on the sea off Swanage in fog, and was subsequently out of the contest.

Quadrant picture library

This picture shows a number of flying boats at the 1920 Monaco seaplane meeting, which preceded that year's Schneider contest at Venice. On the right is a Savoia S.12, basically similar to the aircraft which won the Trophy for Italy in the poorly attended 1920 contest.

Quadrant picture library

Above: The Supermarine Sea Lion II of 1922. This aircraft, flown by Supermarine test pilot Henri Biard, won that year's contest, so depriving the Italians of a third and final victory. This aircraft shared a number of features with the Sea Lion I of 1919. It too was developed from a Baby, and had a 450hp Napier Lion engine. Its fuselage was about 2 feet shorter, though, and this, together with a four-bladed propeller of increased diameter, resulted in an increased swing when the throttle was opened. The rudder was therefore enlarged, as can be seen in the picture, to counteract this effect. *Quadrant picture library*

Below: A hive of activity in Sammy Saunders' Cowes hanger, 1923. The aircraft in the foreground is the French CAMS (Chantiers Aéro-Maritime de la Seine) 38. It was flown by pilot Hurel in the contest, but had to land prematurely near Selsey Bill with a badly vibrating Hispano-Suiza engine. In the background is one of the American Curtiss CR-3 racers. *Quadrant picture library*

Test pilot Alphonse Duhamel, in front of his Latham L.1 flying boat. The Latham flying boats (there were two at the 1923 contest) were built by the French firm Société Industrielle de Caudebec-en-Caux. This particular aircraft never reached the start line of the 1923 contest, suffering a failed magneto in one of its Lorraine-Dietrich engines. *Quadrant picture library*

Presumably Duhamel taxying his Latham L.1 in what appears to be the River Medina, leading into Cowes on the Isle of Wight. The two Lorraine-Dietrich engines can be seen, as can the low 'sit' in the water. *Quadrant picture library*

Above: The aircraft which upset the applecart at the 1923 contest – the American Curtiss CR-3. This is the aircraft of US Navy Lieutenant David Rittenhouse, who won the Trophy that year. The overall streamlined effect of the twin-pontoon arrangement is apparent, especially when compared with the pictures of the French Latham and CAMS flying boats. This aircraft, with a wheeled undercarriage, had also won the 1921 Pulitzer Trophy in the United States. The aircraft had brass radiators fitted flush with the wings, and a metal propeller able to cope with the power from the Curtiss D-12 engine better than a wooden one. Everything about the aircraft is neat and tidy – both it and the second CR-3 caused a storm. *Quadrant picture library*

Right: The Supermarine Sea Lion III, 1923. Henri Biard did his desperate best to beat the Americans with their super-streamlined CR-3s. But a comparison of the frontal area of this aircraft with that of the CR-3 shows he could never have achieved this. He finished third. His speed was faster than any previous Schneider winner, but it was still nearly 20 miles per hour slower than the Americans. *Quadrant picture library*

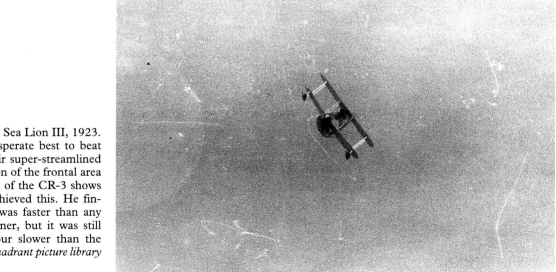

7

The well-known picture of Lieutenant James Doolittle, of the US Army, on the pontoon of one of the Curtiss R3C aircraft from the 1925 contest. Doolittle was a veteran of many US air races in addition to competing in the Schneider contest of this particular year. This photograph seems to be one of a whole set taken at or near the time of the race, with each of the US pilots posing with the same aircraft. Doolittle won the contest, but this was the last US victory in the series. It is interesting to compare this aircraft with the Curtiss CR-3 of two years previously. Although both obviously Curtiss racers, the R3C is clearly more advanced than its predecessor. Engine power has increased by about 50%, maximum speed by about 140 miles per hour. *Author's collection*

A contemporary postcard of the Gloster IV. Designer Harry Folland stuck with the biplane configuration longer than any other Schneider designer. He designed the Gloster IV for the 1927 Schneider contest, at Venice. It was his last biplane Schneider design (following it with the Gloster VI) and so was the ultimate biplane racer. Three were built, this one being N222, showing the cruciform tail introduced to improve directional stability. It was not used in the 1927 contest, but was retained, slightly altered, as a practice aircraft for the 1929 and 1931 High Speed Flights. *Author's collection*

A photograph demonstrating what the Schneider Trophy contests were to become – all-out speed competitions. This is the Macchi M.39, designed by Macchi's designer Mario Castoldi for the 1926 contest, held in the United States. The streamlining used on the aircraft is self-evident. The wings carry the radiators needed to cool the Fiat AS.2 engine and they can be seen along the top surfaces. As with just about every Schneider racer, the visibility forward for the pilot is non-existent. This aircraft achieved just over 272 miles per hour during a successful world seaplane record attempt.

Author's collection

Another contemporary postcard, this time publicising Pratt's petrol and featuring the Supermarine S.5. Inset is Flight Lieutenant Sidney Webster, who won the 1927 contest in the S.5 featured. The aircraft was designed by R.J. Mitchell, and had a number of design changes over its predecessor, the S.4, which crashed during practice during the 1925 contest. L.P. Coombes was based at the Marine Aircraft Experimental Establishment and was involved with the testing of the three S.5s, as well as the other British aircraft (the Gloster IVs and the Short Crusader) before the contest in Venice. He describes some of the design and testing of the S.5: 'Research [on the S.5] was undertaken at RAE [Royal Aircraft Establishment, Farnborough] and NPL [National Physical Laboratory] and at the maker's works [Supermarine]. The first objective was to reduce air resistance. It was found that the external radiators had a high resistance amounting to about one third of the total drag of the whole aircraft. This loss was almost totally eliminated by fitting radiators which formed part of the skin of the aircraft. Engine development played an important part, both in increasing power and reducing air drag. Both the Supermarine and Gloster aircraft used the Napier Lion which had three banks of cylinders in line. It was found possible to reduce the height of the cylinders and to house the auxiliaries behind them. The result was a reduction of frontal area of nearly 25%. Weight was also reduced to 900lbs.'

Author's collection

How to transport a racing seaplane. These are two Italian Macchi M.52s, on the water at Venice on their launch craft. The Macchi M.52 was a development of the earlier M.39 which had been victorious in the previous year's contest. Basically the aircraft was restyled to accept a much more powerful Fiat engine, the 1,000hp AS.3. Main airframe differences were a slimmer fuselage, a swept-back wing (visible on the rear aircraft) and increased areas for the control surfaces. Three of these aircraft competed at Venice in 1927, all unfortunately retiring before finishing. *Quadrant picture library*

Another shot of one of the Gloster IVs of 1927. The symmetrical nature of the tail is clearly evident here, the 'fin' on the underside of the fuselage being added for additional directional stability. The pilot in the boat, on the far right of the picture, is Flight Lieutenant Kinkhead, whose aircraft this was in the contest. He eventually retired on the sixth lap, after which it was found that the shaft of the propeller was close to breaking away completely. *Quadrant picture library*

The Short Crusader, the only radial-engined aircraft to be entered for a Schneider contest. The exposed cylinder heads of the Bristol Mercury engine can be seen in this picture. They were normally covered with individual 'helmets' in an attempt to reduce their aerodynamic drag. The pilot from the 1927 High Speed Flight assigned to fly this aircraft was Flying Officer H.M. Schofield. In his book *High Speed and Other Flights* he mentions his doubts about whether the aircraft could compete with the Supermarine S.5s and Gloster IVs. The rudder appeared to be too small, and on its first flight after delivery to Felixstowe proved troublesome to land. Worse was to come. The aileron control cables had become frayed, and before transit to Venice, new ones were spliced onto the old. However, the fork ends were reversed so that the controls could only be rigged incorrectly. On his first flight at Venice, Schofield, attempting to correct a wing drop, crashed into the sea. Fortunately, he suffered only concussion.

Quadrant picture library

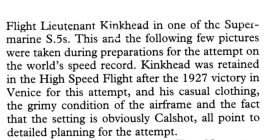

Flight Lieutenant Kinkhead in one of the Supermarine S.5s. This and the following few pictures were taken during preparations for the attempt on the world's speed record. Kinkhead was retained in the High Speed Flight after the 1927 victory in Venice for this attempt, and his casual clothing, the grimy condition of the airframe and the fact that the setting is obviously Calshot, all point to detailed planning for the attempt.

Times Newspapers

How not to get your feet wet. Although the method of carrying pilots ashore is familiar, this shot of Kinkhead is less so. This aircraft was not used at Venice in the contest itself. The corrugated strips along the fuselage side are the oil coolers. This shot also shows the poor visibility available to pilots through the cockpit hood.　　　　　　　　　　　　　　　　　　　　　　　*Times Newspapers*

The wreckage of Kinkhead's S.5, photographed by Harold Andrews, who was with the RAF High Speed Flight at the time of the record attempt. The technique used in attempting world speed records was to dive to the required height before entering the measured distance over which the record was timed. Kinkhead, perhaps distracted by the calm surface of the sea, didn't pull out of his dive.　　*Harold Andrews*

Part Two: 1929 & 1931

Many of the photographs in this section are from the collection of Harold Andrews, who was a member of the ground crew of the RAF High Speed Flights of both 1929 and 1931. This shot is up the slip way at Calshot, with one of the Supermarine S.6s being prepared for a practice at the top.

Harold Andrews

A shot of S.6 N248 from a contemporary postcard. The High Speed Flight referred to the aircraft by their registration numbers, a practice mimicked in this book. This aircraft was flown in the 1929 contest by Flying Officer Richard Atcherley. In fact, he was disqualified for cutting a turning point after losing his goggles. The aircraft was refurbished and upgraded into an S.6A for the 1931 contest, and survives today in the Southampton Hall of Aviation.

via Harold Andrews

One of the Supermarine S.5s from 1927, now in 1929 livery. This is in fact Webster's winning aircraft from 1927. In 1929, the S.5s were practice aircraft for the High Speed Flight, although one of them did in fact compete in the contest. Squadron Leader Orlebar, the captain of the High Speed Flight, made some interesting comparisons between the S.5 and the Gloster IVs, also used for practice. 'Being a low wing monoplane, the S.5 has no top wing to get in the way, and so the view is rather better than in the Gloster's, but there is certainly no spare room in the cockpit ... The controls are as good as the Gloster's ... but there is more change of trim between engine on and off.'

Harold Andrews

Left: One of the consequences of working in the sea was that, after every flight, the aircraft had to be hosed down. Here, S.6 N247 dries off in front of the hanger.
Harold Andrews

Below: The entire High Speed Flight of 1929, photographed in November of that year. Harold Andrews is seated on the back row, third in from the left. In the centre is R.J. Mirchell, who designed all Supermarine's Schneider racers. To his left is Squadron Leader Orlebar, the Flight Captain. In front of them are the rest of the officers: from left to right, Moon (engineering officer), Waghorn (without the moustache he wore during the actual contest), Atcherley and Stainforth. This picture was probably taken just before the Flight moved back to Felixstowe, to the Marine Aircraft Experimental Establishment.
via Harold Andrews

The lot of the High Speed Flight Ground Crew. In addition to working on the aircraft, they also manhandled boats. This party may well be off to sweep The Solent of debris before a practice flight.
Harold Andrews

A superb study of the Supermarine S.6. This is the winning aircraft from 1929, and it also took the world's speed record too. The corrugations are again the oil cooler, which carried the hot oil back to the tail. Inside the fin the oil ran down to the bottom of the tail through channels, and was then pumped back along the underside of the aircraft. Water radiators were set into the wings.
Harold Andrews

Calshot Spit from the air, 1929. The far hanger was the base for the Schneider aircraft. Although aircraft are visible on the station, no racing seaplanes are out. The castle is visible behind the long, white hanger, and the main slipway into the water is hidden beyond it. Most of these buildings, and all the hangers, still exist.
Harold Andrews

Another shot of S.5 N220. Calshot Castle is in the background, and has not changed to this day. *via Harold Andrews*

Yet more straining for the ground crew. Presumably a racing seaplane is on the other end of the halyard. Stan Hall, another member of the 1931 ground crew, explained that normally a winch was used to haul the aircraft onto the slipway, requiring a three day training session on its use. Perhaps these aircraftmen had not yet received their training! *Harold Andrews*

Above left: Harold Andrews is the middle airman of the three. The other two are 'DR' and 'Jack'. Andrews cannot remember what had happened to Jack! *Above right:* Tam and Darkie, taken by Harold Andrews, Felixstowe, 1930. The High Speed Flight moved back to Suffolk at the end of 1929, and awaited the new designs for the 1931 contest. *Below:* Another group shot of members of the High Speed Flight, in 1930. Ground crew comprised the best aircraftman in each fighter squadron. Andrews came from 56 Squadron, then equipped with Armstrong-Whitworth Siskins. There are no names with this picture. *All Harold Andrews*

The impressive British line-up for the 1929 contest. Every aircraft available to the High Speed Flight at Calshot is in this picture. Left to right, they are: Supermarine S.5, Gloster VI, Supermarine S.6, Gloster IV, S.6, Gloster VI and S.5. The S.6s used Rolls-Royce 'R' engines, the others various types of Napier Lion. The Gloster VIs were plagued with fuel supply problems particularly in the turns. *Harold Andrews*

Harold Andrews is in the cap, the other two aircraftmen being 'DR' and 'Jack'. Behind them is one of the S.5s, used for practice by the new intake of pilots. Orlebar's dry comment was 'we have generally had at least one going'. *Harold Andrews*

One of the strangest designs entered for a Schneider contest – the Italian Savoia-Marchetti S.65. Powered by two Isotta-Fraschini Asso engines in tandem, with the rear engine driving a pusher propeller, the aircraft also had twin booms supporting the tail. The pilot sat between the engines, and as can be seen in this picture, the whole effect was to produce a streamlined, if unconventional, aircraft. However, engine cooling problems precluded it flying at the contest itself, although it was retained in the Italian team for morale purposes.

Harold Andrews

The scene at Calshot during the lead-up to the 1929 contest, at the press day. The journalists are assembled to the right of the picture and it looks as if they are interviewing either one of the pilots or an official. The aircraft is Supermarine S.6 N247.

Harold Andrews

A nice shot of one of the S.6s from 1929. Ground (water?) crew members manhandle the aircraft in preparation to haul it out of the water. In the background is the launch carrying one of the pilots and, judging by their civilian clothes, Supermarine officials.
Harold Andrews

The practice Supermarine S.5 from 1929. This was the sister to the one flown by Flight Lieutenant D'Arcy Greig in the 1929 contest.
Harold Andrews

One of the Gloster VIs built for the 1929 contest, from a contemporary postcard. This was designer H.P. Folland's first racing monoplane, but he retained the Napier Lion engine, in contrast with rival Reginald Mitchell at Supermarine, who switched to Rolls-Royce. The three banks of the 'broad arrow' shape of the Lion are clearly visible, forming the outer surfaces of the engine cowlings. The picture also shows how these racing seaplanes were transported into The Solent on lighters, special seaplane tenders towed behind launches.
via Harold Andrews

A Gloster VI, showing just how streamlined these aircraft were. Folland designed the wing of the Gloster VI with the roots thinner than the mid-section. This was to give the aircraft more control in the roll at slower speeds (such as on landing). Contemporary newspapers, as well as Harold Andrews, described these aircraft as the most beautiful of all the Schneider racers. *Harold Andrews*

Supermarine N247 on the water. This picture shows the general layout of the design well.   *Harold Andrews*

The same aircraft, N247, on its beaching dolly. In this picture it seems to have a different propeller. The RAF High Speed Flight, with the Supermarine engineers, tried and tested a whole range of propellers, to find the one that combined the best take-off performance with the highest speed flat out in the air. Some were of such an extreme pitch that the aircraft never left the water.

Harold Andrews

The appeal of the Schneider contests can be gleaned from this picture. An estimated one million spectators witnessed the 1929 contest. Here, one of the Italian M.67s hurtles past the Southsea crowds at around 360 miles per hour. In those days, everyone wore a hat.
Times Newspapers

A Gloster VI is run up on the slip, whilst a Supermarine S.6 flies over Calshot Castle. Persistent problems with the fuel flow in the Glosters led to their withdrawal from the final British line-up for the 1929 contest. The pilot is just visible in the Gloster cockpit, hunched forward in front of his engine instruments, probably checking the water temperature gauge. *Author's collection*

The same Gloster VI. Two aircraft were built, this one sporting blue floats and gold fuselage and wings. It was named Golden Arrow.
Author's collection

Above: The second Gloster VI. The fitter on the step ladder at the propeller has that most essential of tools in his overall pocket, a ball-pein hammer. *Times Newspapers*

Left: The three British pilots who represented Britain in the 1929 contest. From the left, Flight Lieutenant D'Arcy Greig, Flying Officer H.R. Waghorn and Flying Officer Richard 'Batchy' Atcherley. Greig flew the Supermarine S.5, Waghorn S.6 N247 and Atcherley S.6 N248. Waghorn won, but miscounted his laps, and landed out of fuel during an extra, unnecessary eighth lap. Atcherley lost his goggles in the aircraft slipstream, and in keeping his head tucked inside the cockpit, missed one of the turning points and was disqualified.

Times Newspapers

Above: Flight Lieutenant George Stainforth in Gloster VI N250. Stainforth elected to fly the Gloster, and so never flew in the 1929 contest because of the fuel flow problems suffered by the aircraft. However, he did take the world's speed record in N249 after the contest. *Times Newspapers*

Right: Italian team members from 1929. From the left, Warrant Officer Dal Molin (who flew the Macchi M.52R), General Italo Balbo, the Italian Air Minister, Lieutenant Giovanni Monti (Macchi M.67) and Lieutenant Remo Cadringher (Macchi M.67). These were the pilots who were selected to form the team of three which actually competed. *Times Newspapers*

Left: Monti being escorted from his aircraft after being scolded by hot cooling water from his Macchi M.67. His scalded wrists are already bandaged.

Times Newspapers

Below: The RAF High Speed Flight for the 1929 contest, with the Prince of Wales and one of the hack Gloster IVs. Left to right are Waghorn, Stainforth, Orlebar, Prince Edward, D'Arcy Greig, Atcherley, Wing Commander Sidney Smith (overall organiser of the 1929 contest) and Moon, the engineering officer. On the right is 'Nobby' Clarke, a technical officer attached to the Flight from Farnborough.

Author's collection

Above: Waghorn climbs into his S.6 for the start of his speed trial in the 1929 contest. The wind is up, giving just the right amount of lop on the Solent waves. A calm surface was of no use in getting these seaplanes into the air, because of the suction on the undersides of the floats, and too much rough water was equally unsuitable. The power of the Rolls-Royce engine was so great that on opening the throttle the aircraft slewed round under the torque. So, the pilots turned their aircraft out of wind before opening up, so that as flying speed was reached, the aircraft had turned back into wind. The pilots now had sufficient speed to be able to control the aircraft with the rudder, and the take-off could be achieved.

Author's collection

Right: Lord Thompson, the Secretary of State for Air, with Captain Canaveri and Lieutenant Monti of the Italian team, just one week before the contest. Thompson was later to die in the R.101 airship crash. *Author's collection*

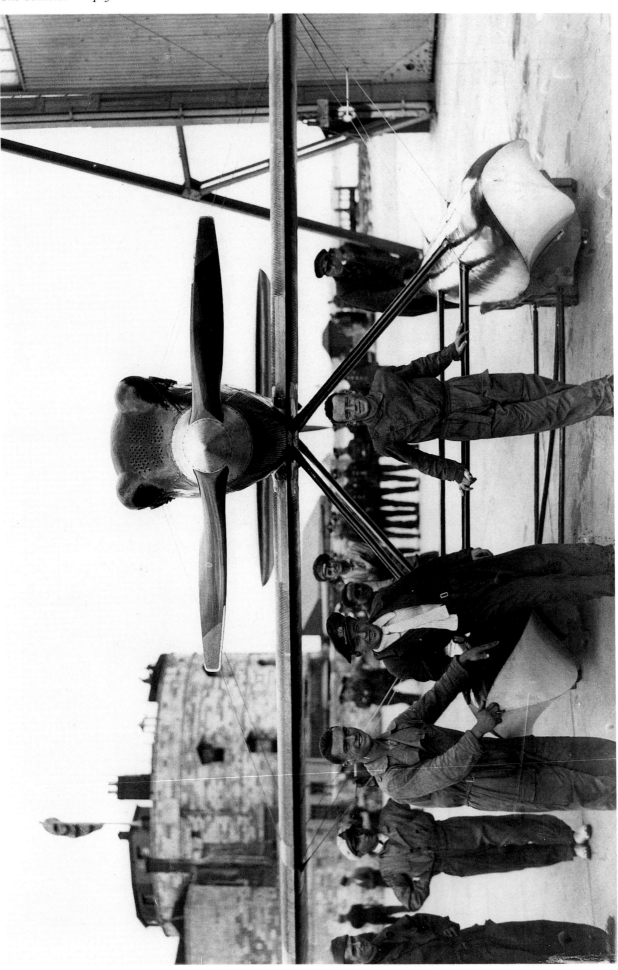

Another picture demonstrating how streamlined these aircraft were. This is the Italian Macchi M.52R. This was a restyled upgrade of the M.52 from 1927, with shortened wings and reduced frontal area. The engine was a Fiat AS.3 delivering 1,000hp. In the contest itself this aircraft was flown by pilot Dal Molin who finished second between Waghorn in the S.6 and D'Arcy Greig in the S.5.

Author's collection

Lord Thompson's turn with the RAF High Speed Flight. Waghorn is sporting a very smart pair of sunglasses.   *Author's collection*

Italian pilot Dal Molin being carried ashore from the Macchi M.52. This aircraft was nicknamed the Moor of Venice because of its overall stained, oil-streaked appearance, and because it had competed at Venice.   *Author's collection*

Above left: General Italo Balbo, Italian Under-Secretary for Air (with stick) with the captain of the Italian team from 1929, General Bernasconi. Balbo was the overall leader of his country's team, and later found world fame for leading an armada of Siai-Marchetti S.55s across the Atlantic. One of the people he spoke with whilst at Calshot was Aircraftman T.E. Shaw, better known as T.E. Lawrence – Lawrence of Arabia. Lawrence had enlisted in the RAF in the 1920s and was working on the development of high speed seaplane launches, some of which were used during the Schneider contests.   *Author's collection*

Above right: Captain A. Canaveri of the 1929 Italian Schneider team. He was not selected for the final team which actually took part in that year's contest.   *Author's collection*

Left: Italian pilot Dal Molin on one of the RAF launches. During one of the practice flights in one of the Macchi M.52Rs, his aircraft developed a leak in one of its floats, probably after hitting an object whilst taxying. On landing the float started to ship water, resulting in the RAF rescue party.

Author's collection

A superb view of the Italian Macchi M.67 and M.52R on their lighter, *en route* to their moorings for the watertightness tests. Race number 10, the M.67, was Monti's aircraft, the other Dal Molin's M.52R.   *Author's collection*

The second Macchi M.67, this one being the aircraft of Remo Cadringher, and carrying a three-bladed propeller. The pilot on this occasion, though, is Monti. The picture was taken just a few days before the contest. The highly polished finish on the fuselage and floats can be clearly seen.   *Author's collection*

Flying Officer Giovanni Monti in the cockpit of the Macchi M.52 practice aircraft. Streaked with oil and, as can be seen in a generally dishevelled state, this aircraft is the Moor of Venice. The photograph was taken exactly one week before the 1929 contest.

Author's collection

Right: Lieutenant Remo Cadringher, who piloted one of the two Macchi M67s. The new Macchis were the biggest threat to the British and Cadringher's take-off in the contest was closely watched. Once airborne, his engine started to emit thick black smoke, and he landed at the end of his first lap, overcome from the fumes.
Author's collection

Below: The winner of the 1929 Schneider Trophy contest, H.R.D. Waghorn, in the cockpit of his Supermarine S.6. Despite the racing number, he was the first to start the contest itself. *Author's collection*

Monti again, this time in the new M.67, taxiing out for a practice a few days before the contest. The liner is the *Majestic*. This picture shows nicely how ships and aircraft had to share The Solent. Ships were a particular hazard, not so much from the vessels themselves but from their wash, which was quite sufficient to flip the delicate racers over.

Author's collection

This is the watertightness and navigability test, the day before the contest proper, in 1929. D'Arcy Greig in the Supermarine S.5 is taxying off to commence his short flight and landing prior to the mooring out. Monti's Macchi M.67 sits on the lighter, next to go. The S.5 had finished second, piloted by Worsley, in Venice two years previously. *Author's collection*

The pilot is Monti again, the aircraft an M.67 and the battleship looming in the background is HMS *Iron Duke*. As can be seen from the direction of flight, *Iron Duke* had got in Monti's way. The navigability tests required two landings. Monti did his first ahead of the bow, his second astern the great ship. *Author's collection*

A supremely atmospheric shot of one of the Supermarine S.6s, together with designer R.J. Mitchell. This is N248, which was Atcherley's aircraft in the 1929 contest and Snaith's (as the upgraded S.6A) in 1931. The pitot tube on the starboard wing was removed for the actual contest. The guard is for real.
Author's collection

Left: The leader of the 1929 Italian team, Colonel Bernasconi.
Author's collection

Right: Lieutenant Giovanni Monti, pilot of one of the two Macchi M.67s of 1929.
Author's collection

The competitor which never was – the American Al Williams and his Mercury racer. Following the 1926 Schneider contest, the American government stopped funding Schneider entries in particular and service pilots racing in general, preferring instead to absorb what had been learned over the years of competitive flying. So, it was left to private investors funding private entries to continue American interest. Williams, winner of the 1923 Pulitzer race, was the most persistent, having also attempted to enter the 1927 Schneider contest. Built by the Naval Air Factory at Philadelphia, the Mercury was powered by a Packard engine. However, Williams experienced extreme difficulty in getting off the water in test flights and it was discovered that the Packard was underpowered for the airframe. Finally, the Navy Department withdrew its offer of free travel across the Atlantic, and the challenge languished.
Author's collection

Above left: The wreckage of Gloster IVB N223, crashed by John Boothman in practice on December 19th 1930. Boothman was unhurt. The day started foggy but cleared later in the morning. In fact, Squadron Leader Orlebar was scheduled to fly that day, but was too busy and sanctioned Boothman to take the aircraft up. Whilst airborne the fog rolled back. Believing he had a problem with the elevator, and disoriented by the fog, Boothman hit the water with a bang, breaking the aircraft on impact. Boothman and Gloster went to the bottom of Felixstowe harbour – as Orlebar commented: 'there was proof ... because his shoes were covered in mud.' *Harold Andrews*

Above right: Another shot, taken by Harold Andrews, of the wrecked Gloster. These are the floats and the bracing wires are obviously mangled. *Harold Andrews*

Below: The first two digits of the Gloster's registration N223 are visible on the wrecked fin in this picture. It seems astonishing that a pilot could survive such a crash, with the additional effects of submersion, unscathed. *Harold Andrews*

Above: Spectators at Calshot. It is interesting to speculate who these people are, as Calshot was closed to the general public. Perhaps they are relatives of the High Speed Flight personnel. Even the dog is interested!
Times Newspapers

Right: Another shot from Harold Andrews of ground crew members on one of the lighters. The tail of one of the S.6s is in the foreground on the right, in focus. The engine cowling and propeller are visible behind the aircraftmen. Andrews is second from the right.
Harold Andrews

41

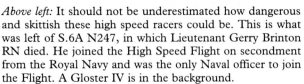

Above left: It should not be underestimated how dangerous and skittish these high speed racers could be. This is what was left of S.6A N247, in which Lieutenant Gerry Brinton RN died. He joined the High Speed Flight on secondment from the Royal Navy and was the only Naval officer to join the Flight. A Gloster IV is in the background.

Harold Andrews

Above right: The engine bay of Brinton's wrecked S.6A. The force of the impact with the water can be imagined by the severity of the damage. *Harold Andrews*

Right: A very poignant picture of Brinton's wrecked aircraft. Brinton took the S.6A out for his first flight on the type on 18th August 1931. He was briefed on the aircraft's characteristics on take-off, which were a tendency to porpoise unless the control column was hauled back, a technique contrary to any pilot's instinct. Unfortunately, Brinton allowed the aircraft to smack onto the water a number of times, before it bounced about 30 feet into the air and crashed. When the aircraft was later recovered, Brinton's body was apparently missing. In fact, the force of the impact had forced his body back up the fuselage. This picture shows how the fuselage skin was peeled open to remove the body.

Harold Andrews

Supermarine S.5 N220. This aircraft won at Venice in 1927. This picture could be 1929 or 1931 – the aircraft was used as a practice machine in both contests.   *Harold Andrews*

Gloster VI N249, 1931. By this time, the magnificent Glosters had been reduced to practice status.   *Harold Andrews*

Another shot by Harold Andrews, of S.5 N220, with Nick and John ...   *Harold Andrews*

The hack Fairey Flycatcher from 1931. After John Boothman had completed the flyover, to take the Schneider Trophy permanently, there was a lull whilst the second S.6B was prepared for George Stainforth for a world's speed record attempt. This lull was filled by Leonard Snaith, who entertained the crowds around The Solent with a display of aerobatics in this aircraft.

Harold Andrews

... and the S.5 again, with 'Stainless'.   *Harold Andrews*

Gloster VI N249 being prepared at night. With the wings removed, the sleek profile of this beautiful aircraft becomes apparent. Compare this with the profile of the Supermarine S.6B elsewhere.   *Harold Andrews*

Above: One of the Gloster IVs from 1927, which were used as practice aircraft in both 1929 and 1931. Each of the Glosters as originally built were slightly different from each other, and so were designated Gloster IV, IVA and IVB. After the 1927 contest they were returned to Gloster's for alteration and conversion to trainers. This is the Gloster IVA, with 900 horse power Napier Lion engine. The engine is being run up but there appears to be no pilot at the controls.   *Harold Andrews*

Left: An interesting shot by Harold Andrews of S.6A N247 on its lighter. Although the camera was focused on the tail, the slimness of the fuselage is evident. Mitchell basically fitted pilot and airframe behind the contours of the Rolls-Royce 'R' engine.
Harold Andrews

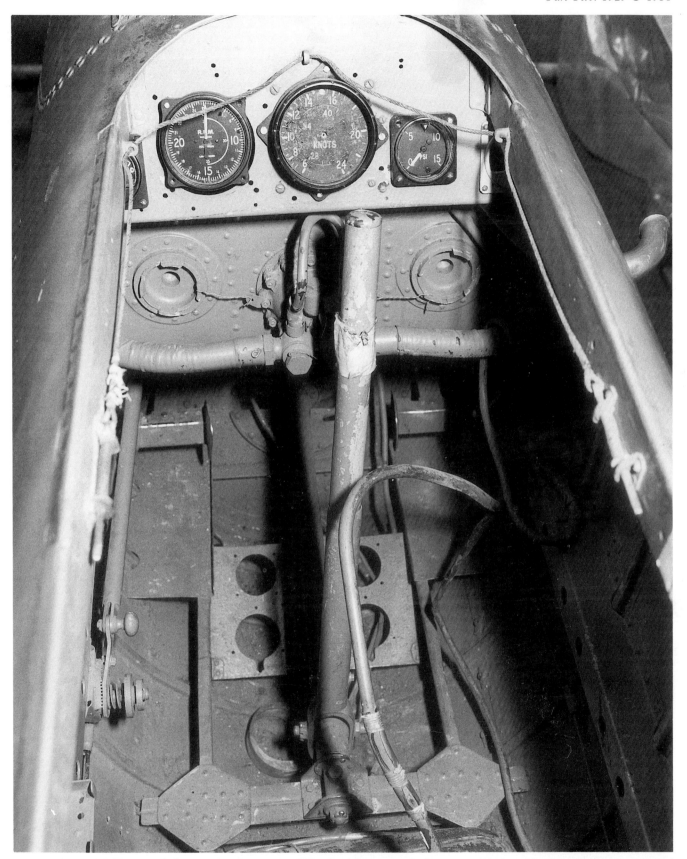

In 1984 the British Hovercraft Corporation (now part of Westland Aerospace Ltd) was commissioned by the Southampton Hall of Aviation to refurbish its Supermarine S.6. The aircraft is in fact N248, used in the 1929 contest, and also upgraded to S.6A standard (with a more powerful version of the Rolls-Royce 'R' engine) for 1931. The work allowed detailed investigation of how these aircraft were designed and constructed. This picture shows the instrument panel and control column. The large central instrument is the air speed indicator. To its left is the engine speed indicator, and on the right the oil pressure gauge. The cable running above them is the canopy latch release cable. The 'inverted U' shaped pipe beneath the air speed indicator is the petrol header tank vent pipe. On the floor is an instrument panel with four holes in it. It contained the oil inlet temperature gauge, boost pressure gauge and fuel pressure gauge. The pilot's seat (Atcherley in 1929, Snaith in 1931) is at the bottom of the picture.   *Westland Aerospace Ltd*

Left: The engine bay of the S.6A, looking back towards the cockpit. The small tank at the top of the fuselage, immediately in front of the cockpit with two inlet holes, is the steam header tank.

Below: The port and starboard oil coolers. These were fixed along the fuselage sides to take the hot oil from the engine to the tail, for cooling.

Westland Aerospace Ltd

Another cockpit shot. The upper lever is the throttle control, and its control rod is also visible. Beneath it is the mixture control lever. The old-fashioned electrical switch tucked under the top fuselage longeron is the ignition switch! Just visible on the instrument panel, top left, is the coolant temperature gauge. John Boothman flew his S.6B to this gauge, not to his airspeed indicator. The circular object to the left of the control column is a petrol header tank filler and filter – there was one on each side. The left rudder pedal is also visible.

Westland Aerospace Ltd

Above: The complete aircraft in 1931 – S.6A N248. The weather conditions look as damp out of the water as in it, in this picture. *Times Newspapers*

Left: The pilots of the 1931 High Speed Flight, *en route* to the start line. From the left are Flying Officer Leonard Snaith, Flight Lieutenant Frank Long and Flight Lieutenant John Boothman. The order of flying was Boothman in S.6B S1595, Snaith in the safe S.6A N248, and Long in the second S.6B, S1596. In the event, Boothman completed his flight successfully.

Times Newspapers

Above: The victorious aircraft back on dry land. The enthusiastic crowd of VIPs follows behind. *Times Newspapers*

Right: The victor – John Boothman is hoisted aloft by the ground crew. Harold Andrews is second from left, Stan Hall is waving the cap. Boothman was a popular officer. According to Eileen Phillip, whose guardian he was, he was also a great practical joker. According to her, the only time he was afraid whilst flying was later in his career, on a trip from Egypt to Iraq, when the Dove he was flying entered icing conditions. It seems he took the S.6B in his stride.
Times Newspapers

This is Harold Andrews' own picture of John Boothman just after his successful flight. Boothman himself looks slightly bemused by all the attention, although he was extremely proud to have won the Trophy for Britain.   *Harold Andrews*

Following Boothman's successful flyover for the Schneider Trophy, on Sunday September 13th, 1931, George Stainforth made a successful attempt on the world's speed record in the second S.6B. Here is pilot and aircraft. His average speed over four runs was 379.05 miles per hour, achieved with the standard competition engine fitted in the aircraft. On September 29th, with a special sprint engine fitted to S.1595, Stainforth did four runs averaging 408.8 miles per hour – the first man to exceed 400 miles per hour.
                    Times Newspapers

In 1987, at the Battle of Britain at Home day at RAF Abingdon, the anniversary of Britain's 1927 Venice victory was commemorated. The Supermarine S.6A from the Southampton Hall of Aviation, now completely restored, was moved to the airfield, as was the Schneider Trophy itself, under guard, from the Science Museum. *Author's collection*

The celebrations – the High Speed Flight dinner following the victory. Stan Hall is facing the camera on the left, Orlebar is standing in the centre at the back.

Harold Andrews

Fifty years on – Webster, Long and D'Arcy Greig at the 50th anniversary commemoration at Calshot.

Keith Wilson

The Schneider Trophy. The winged figure represents speed and flight, the figures in the waves the sea. Octopi and crabs adorn the base. This magnificent Trophy rested in the Royal Aero Club before being presented to London's Science Museum where it is now on public show. According to Eileen Phillip, Boothman, by virtue of having won the Trophy, was the only person allowed to hang his hat on it while it was at the Royal Aero Club. *Author's collection*

Acknowledgements

This book would not have been possible without the photographs and memories of Harold Andrews and Stan Hall. Of the other people with whom I have spoken or corresponded over a number of years, special thanks are due to Martin Snaith, L.P. Coombes and Eileen Phillip. Peter Murton and Mike Tagg of the Royal Air Force Museum, Hendon have also been very helpful on a number of occasions. And it was my privilege to have met Group Captain Leonard Snaith and Air Commodore D. D'Arcy Greig. Finally, a word of thanks to Dermot McKeone, Marcus Palliser and Jackie Boxall, for providing the business context which introduced me to the Schneider Trophy in the first place; and to my wife Jane, for putting up with this obsession for the past six years.

Sources

There are a large number of books on the Schneider Trophy, and most general books on aviation include a section on the contests. The main references for this book are as follows:

The Speed Seekers, Thomas G. Foxworth, Haynes Publishing 1989

Schneider Trophy Aircraft 1913-1931, Derek N. James, Putnam 1981

The Schneider Trophy Races, Ralph Barker, Airlife 1981

Speed, T.S. Denham, The Pilot Press 1929

High-Speed and Other Flights, H.M. Schofield, John Hamilton, publication date unknown

Schneider Trophy, A.H. Orlebar, Seeley Service & Co 1933

Also contemporary issues of *Flight* and *The Aeroplane*.